# You, Me, And Everything In Between.

A Journey through Love and Loss

Naga Sanjay

BookLeaf Publishing
India | USA | UK

Copyright © Naga Sanjay
All Rights Reserved.

This book has been self-published with all reasonable efforts taken to make the material error-free by the author. No part of this book shall be used, reproduced in any manner whatsoever without written permission from the author, except in the case of brief quotations embodied in critical articles and reviews.

The Author of this book is solely responsible and liable for its content including but not limited to the views, representations, descriptions, statements, information, opinions, and references ["Content"]. The Content of this book shall not constitute or be construed or deemed to reflect the opinion or expression of the Publisher or Editor. Neither the Publisher nor Editor endorse or approve the Content of this book or guarantee the reliability, accuracy, or completeness of the Content published herein and do not make any representations or warranties of any kind, express or implied, including but not limited to the implied warranties of merchantability, fitness for a particular purpose.

The Publisher and Editor shall not be liable whatsoever...

Made with ❤ on the BookLeaf Publishing Platform
www.bookleafpub.in
www.bookleafpub.com

# Dedication

*To the people who taught me how and how not to love.*

*Thank you.*

# Preface

Have you ever met someone and felt the entire map of your life shift? Have you wondered what it means to love so completely that the other person becomes both your home and your exile? What is it about heartbreak that teaches us more about ourselves than happiness ever could?

Love and loss are not opposites. They are two sides of the same breath. Love shows us what we're capable of feeling; loss teaches us that we're capable of surviving. There is a quiet beauty in both—in the way we bloom for another, and in the way we learn to bloom for ourselves.

These poems were written over 8 years, tracking the contours of a love that shaped me profoundly. They move through stages: the euphoria of meeting, the depth of connection, the confusion and conflict that tested us, the quiet acceptance of endings, and finally, the transformation that follows heartbreak.

This is a chronological narrative and an emotional one. Each poem captures a moment—some from memory, some from imagination, all from truth. A realisation. An ache. Together, they form a portrait of what it means to love completely and to survive when that love changes form.

If you've ever loved and lost, if you've felt the full spectrum of what one person can awaken in you, these poems are for you.

# Acknowledgements

# Not the Poet

For once,
I don't want to be the hands
that carves the ache into language.

I want to be the ache.
The soft line someone listens on repeat
because it sounds like something
they forgot they were missing.

I want to be underlined.
Whispered into a collarbone.
Folded into a letter
that someone never sends.

I'm tired of naming beauty.
I want to be it.

For once,
I want to be the thing that lingers.
Not the mouth that lets it go.

For once,
I want to be the poem.
Not the poet.

# The In-Between

I have been in the light,
and I have been in the dark.
But from everything to everywhere,
I prefer to stay in the shadows
from where I can stare into lights.

I have been in the crowd
and I have been in the wards.
But from everything to everywhere,
I prefer to be in a room
from where I can look into the stars.

I have been in love,
and I have been in wars.
But from everything to everywhere,
I prefer to be in her arms
where everything is fair in love and its path.

I have been in the springs
and I have been in the falls.
But from everything to everywhere,
I prefer to stay in Autumns
where I can see leaves growing from the start.

I have been in secrets
and I have been in broadcasts.
But from everything to everywhere,
I prefer to be all unknown
where I can be anyone I want.

# The Heavy Blanket

(Sh)It happens.
Something will go wrong.
once in a lifetime....
For many, much more often...

Imperfect from birth,
mistakes will be made.
Forgiveness is not too rare;
accepting it is.

It means looking
the wound in the eye.
It means admitting
you held the knife.

Guilt is a heavy blanket.
It is easier to stay under it
than to stand up
and be cold for a minute.

To be forgiven is to be seen.
All of it.
The break.
The ugly.

And we are so terrified
of being known.
We trust the ache
more than the cure.

We know how to bleed.
We have forgotten how to heal.

# The Unpromised Light

You stood alone, not out of choice,
but out of something older than longing.

The kind of silence
that doesn't beg to be filled,
just noticed.

Water at your feet,
sky pressing down soft,
you didn't bend.

You bloomed anyway,
in a place no one thought to look
for something living.

Maybe this is what strength looks like,
not loud, not proud,
but a quiet reaching toward a light
that never promised to stay.

I saw you,
and for a moment,
I forgot the world was rushing.

# She doesn't even know

Her laugh isn't light —
it's wildfire.
The kind that dances on dry branches
and dares the forest to feel again.

Her eyes aren't windows.
They are storms just before they break,
velvet grey,
holding back
every word she's never said aloud.

When she speaks,
the air tilts —
like sound itself wants to sit closer.

Time doesn't stop around her.
It kneels.

She walks like her soul
knows every secret the sky ever kept —
like gravity forgot to hold her
just right.

And the cruellest part?

She doesn't even know.
She doesn't see
how every room softens
just because she's in it.

I watch people
fall in love with her
without ever hearing her name.

And I sit here —
selfishly lucky
and silently ruined
to know her this deeply.

# A Mirror of Her Light

When she laughs,
it's not just a sound —
it's a door flying open
in a house I didn't know I lived in.

Her eyes —
god —
they hold stories
I want to spend many lifetimes learning.
Soft storms that never ask permission
to be beautiful.

When she talks,
time forgets its job.
Minutes lean in,
clocks hush,
and the world loses its edge
just to listen.

The way she walks —
like the earth was made to meet her feet,
like every step is poetry
that doesn't need a single word.

And me?
I just stand there,
loving her the way
still water loves the moon.

And I,
the water,
who was only waiting in the dark —
I am now a mirror
of her light.

And I finally,
for the first time,
know my own reason
to shine.

# Not for the crowds

She walks like silence shaped into motion,
like a thought you almost remember.
There's no need to speak when she's near,
even the air listens.

Her eyes don't ask, they understand.
Like she's known pain,
but never let it harden her hands.

She's the kind of woman
you don't notice all at once.
She arrives slowly —
then stays with you,
in the spaces between your thoughts.

Not made for crowds,
but for deep rooms and slow mornings.
She won't burn you with fire —
she'll undo you with softness.

And even in the quietest version of yourself,
you'll find her still there '
not needing to be held —
just... known.

# For You, the World Forgot Its Rules

The coconut grew a third eye —
two weren't enough to understand
how you exist in just one body.

The moon slipped once
just staring at you, missed her cue,
forgot she was supposed to rise—
you were glowing enough.

Rivers reversed to get one more look.
Even my shadow followed you
instead of me.
It knew where the light was.

And my heart?
It learned new rhythms,
beat in iambs and metaphors,
just trying to write you.

The sun started wearing sunglasses at dusk
because your smile made twilight jealous.

Clouds reshaped themselves
into sonnets just to impress you,
but even they drifted apart —
couldn't hold form under your gaze.

Flowers unbloomed at your passing
just to try again —
maybe this time they'd get it right.

My pen ran out of ink
and started bleeding stars —
language wasn't enough.

Even my sleep dreams of you
and wakes me up mid-sentence
asking, "is she real, or just divine mischief?"

Birds asked you for your playlist.
Oceans paused their tides
just to hear what you'd whisper to the wind.

And I,
I stopped being a person
the moment I loved you —
I became a cathedral
echoing with your name.

# My Genesis

I wasn't born a poet.
I didn't know how to hold beauty
without breaking it.

But then you came —
not gently, not like a whisper —
but like colour crashing into grayscale.

You made me feel in volumes
I didn't know I could carry.
And when I couldn't say it,
it spilled through my pen.

You turned every wound into metaphor,
every glance into rhythm.
You weren't just a muse —
you were the moment silence cracked open.

I became an artist the day you taught me
that some emotions don't leave
until you give them a name.

So I wrote you.
And in writing you, I found me.

# A Child's Love

I love you
the way a child loves light;
not needing to own it,
only to stand
where it touches my face.

I love you
with no plan, no proof.
Just the certainty that
you are the most beautiful thing
I've ever looked at
without needing to understand.

There is no ache in it.
No need to be chosen.
Just this quiet joy of
seeing you
and knowing
you exist.

And this is enough
love.

# Idea of 'You'

I'm in love with the idea of you —
The soft myth I made from half-memories,
The echo of your voice where it never lingered long,
The weight of your hand,
Even if it never stayed.

You, in my mind, were always gentler —
Eyes that saw through my noise,
Words that stitched me whole
Without ever asking what broke.

You smiled in all the right places,
Held silence like it was sacred.
You arrived in every version of the future
I dared to believe in.

I built a world around your shadow —
One where the nights weren't so cold,
Where I didn't have to ask to be understood,
Where love didn't flinch
When the lights came on.

Maybe you were never that person.
Maybe I needed you to be.
Maybe I fell in love with a story
That wore your skin like poetry.

And still —
Even knowing all this,
My heart folds back into the shape of you
Like muscle remembering its wound.

Not because you were perfect,
But because the idea of you
Was everything I ever wanted
And never quite had.

# Things you fear the most, like love

It's okay.
I don't expect you to tell me you love me, too.
I just had to let you know that I love you.
You and me both — we both want the warmth.
It's not just about love.

If anything I've learnt so far,
it is that love isn't just romantic or platonic.
It's not a silver lining either.
It's just there.

Sometimes, too thoughtful,
sometimes just practical;
a growing feeling or a fleeting moment;
a man and a woman
or a man and a man.

No, I don't.
I don't understand how exactly it works.
I fear believing that love just happens too quickly.
And I fear to say that it takes time.

Because honestly,
I have been in love at the spur of a moment
and I have taken time to be in love.

But with you,
neither did it just happen
nor it took time.
And this scares me.

What if this is a new kind of love
and requires different ways to hold on to,
but I just processed it
with the knowledge I'd gathered?

I fear to screw it up,
and I can't really tell you.
I think the things you fear the most
have already happened to us.

Like love.

# The Gamble

Some might call it crazy
to say love at first sight is true.
I must come across as cheesy,
but I can't stop wanting you.

Perhaps it's that I'm lonely
and you simply fit the bill.
It turns as a love with reason,
but my heart knows it's for real.

I feel it when I see you.
When you smile, when you laugh.
I wish I could explain it,
but I can't with the mouth open half.

Love shouldn't be a gamble,
but it's time to take a stance.
Accept the risk of asking you
If you'll give me a chance?

# The Bones of This Page

I will write you
so deep into the bones of this page
that even silence will remember
your name.

I will craft your smile
with vowels so tender,
even the ink will blush,
every time it recalls your face.

They will read these lines
and feel the shape of your laugh
in the rhythm.
They will wonder
how light sounds when it speaks,
because I'd have written your voice.

I'll fold your eyes
into metaphors too soft to hold
but too sharp to forget.

Let them try
not to love you
after this.

Let them try
to unsee you,
once the poem is done.

I will write you
so wholly,
they'll ache for the women
they've never met.
And call that ache
love.

# My Promise

I won't be able to bankrupt the stars
or take you to the moon.
Shower the blessings
or paint the sky for you.

But I promise you the nights
we keep on stargazing.
You in the sky,
me into your eyes.

I promise you the days,
we keep on holding hands.
Imagine the feeling you will get,
I swear you will feel blessed.

I promise you the times,
if you ever feel weak,
not in the skies, but the smiles,
I'll paint on your cheeks.

I promise you the darkness
won't be able to touch your soul.
The moonlight will be on your side.
With me, your life will be whole.

# காதல் பித்து

கண்ணிலே கவிபாடும் கவிஞன் தான்
கண் சிவந்தால் சிலையாடும் புலவன் தான்
கதை சொன்னால் கரை நோக்கும் கயல்கள் தான்
இன்று காதல் கனவாலே பித்தானேன்
கடைக் கண்ணாலே.

# The Beauty of 'Almost'

You were never mine,
and maybe that's why
I think of you more tenderly
than those who were.

We were a sentence
that paused
before the period.
A chord
that hummed
but never resolved.

And yet —
how warm the silence felt
between our not-quite words.
How close the air came
to become a touch.

I do not grieve the ending.
There was none.
I grieve the shimmer
of what could have been
if only we had spoken sooner.

Still —
I carry it gently,
this small, glowing ache.

Not all love has to bloom
to be beautiful.

Some just open their eyes
and disappear
like dusk
before the stars arrive.

# The Pain of 'Almost'

I knew.
Of course, I knew.

Every word you didn't say
sounded louder
than the ones you did.

I felt your pause
like a held breath
in a room that never asked for air.

And I —
I almost reached for it.

Almost.

But I had my own silences,
my own ghosts
pacing the floors of my chest.

You were light,
but I wasn't ready
to stop hiding in the dark.

If I could say it back now —
I would.

Not to change it,
but to let you know
you weren't alone
in the almost.

I loved you,
just not enough.

# Rewrite

Can I keep the way we laughed
without remembering how my heart folded itself,
secretly, each time you smiled?

Can I hold on to late-night calls?
The way we spoke like the world
was made of just two voices,
and erase the moment
mine began to tremble?

I'd keep the inside jokes,
the comfort, the ease —
all of it.

Just not the part
where my chest turned into a cage
for a love that could never fly.

If I could, I'd rewrite our story
in ink that doesn't bleed…
Friend, only friend…
and delete
the quiet fall.

# Relive

Give me the beginning,
when your name was just a sound
and not a storm in my chest.

Give me the long talks,
the dumb jokes.
The soft orbit we built
before I knew I was falling.

Let me feel the ache again—
the slow, impossible bloom
of loving you
with nowhere for it to land.

I want the silence after I told you,
the echo of almost that never became more.
The heartbreak, the nights I couldn't sleep,
the tears I hid between sentences—

I want it all.

Because for a while, I got to love you.
And nothing has ever felt more like living.

# A Little

Let's fall in love a little,
in little things we love more.
Every day we come closer,
as we open a new door.

Let the talks go on whole night,
let's sleep with the sun.
Let you stay as a smile on my lips,
as I think it was fun.

Let things go as they are going.
let's not think too much.
Let our eyes kiss from far,
let the fingers feel the touch.

Let's fall in love, A LITTLE..

# Let's just love, love and love

It's ok if we part ways
Let's love this minute more!
Don't care about our sins!
For our love will wash them away.
Let's just love, love and love all day!

It's ok if we aren't meant to be forever
Let's just love and make this night ours!
Don't burden yourself with that fate!
For our love will define its destiny
Let's just love, love and love all this night!

It's ok if our hearts break
Let's just gift them more to each other!
Don't think of that lover's ache!
For the sore nights will soothe in our memories' ease.
Let's just love, love and love as long as we can!

It's ok if we lose this life
Let's just embrace and embalm each other!
Don't fear that death!
For it can only gift us eternal love.
Let's just love, love and love forever and ever!

Hold me tender, kiss me harder
Touch me as yours
And whisper me your love!
Oh, I won't demand anything but you!

Let's just love, love and love
For you and me belong only to 'us!

# Hey Love

You don't fix the world —
but somehow, when you're around,
everything feels lighter.

One message from you
and even my worst days shift,
like the sun decided to try again
just because you spoke.

You love in the quietest ways —
in how you remember what I forget,
in how you listen,
like nothing else in the world matters.

You don't try to save me.
You just stay.
And that means more
than you'll ever know.

When you laugh,
the day softens.
When you look at me,
I feel seen without having to explain a thing.

I never knew love could feel like this —
so gentle,
so constant,
so right.

I'm grateful for you.
More than I say out loud.

— Me

# கவிதை

கதிரவன் உறங்கியதும்
காதினிலோர் குரல்

காத்திருக்கும் இத்தருணங்கள் எல்லாம்
நீர்கண்ட கானலாய்க்
கரைந்தோடும்.

குருவிக்கூடாய் சேகரித்த நினைவலைகள்
உன் கல்லறையும்
தேடி வந்தடையும்.

கயல்விழியவள் அருகினில்
நீ பகிர்ந்த வார்த்தைகள் மட்டும்
கவிதையெனப் பெயர்சூடிக்
காலனையும் ஏமாற்றிடுமே!

# நீ

வண்ணங்கள் அறியா கண்களுக்கும்
கண்களை இழந்த உயிர்களுக்கும்
உயிரின் பொருள் விளங்கா சிலைகளுக்கும்
கவர்ச்சியின் அர்த்தம் நீ...

இசையை அறியா செவிகளுக்கும்
ஓசையின்றி உடையும் மனதிற்கும்
மொழியை இழந்த மௌனத்திற்கும்
ஆறுதலின் அர்த்தம் நீ...

தொடுதலை மறந்த தனிமைக்கும்
உணர்வுகளை இழந்த உடலுக்கும்
கரையைத் தேடும் படகிற்கும்
அடைக்கலத்தின் அர்த்தம் நீ...

ஆம்...
இருள் சூழ்ந்த என் உலகிற்கும்
ஒளியைத் தேடும் என் உயிருக்கும்
காதலின் மொத்த அர்த்தமும் நீ!

# A Presence

The sky is not a canvas.
It's a wound,
bleeding crimson
and purple
and fire
of their memories.

The earth is holding its breath.
The wind is telling a story that
the trees have already forgotten.

Time doesn't bend here.
It stops.
It kneels.

This is where they ran.
A boy and a girl.
Their names are dust.
Their bones are gone.
But their laughter—
it still has a shape.

The air here remembers it.
This isn't just a field.

It's a page they never finished writing.
This isn't just a sunset.
It's their signature.

If you come here when the day is done,
you will feel it.
Not an echo.
A presence.
The love that never learned
how to leave.

# Sunday Morning Ritual

The kettle sings its low hymn
to the quiet light.
You move, a well-known verse,
no questions asked.
You just know.

You pour the amber steam.
Two sugars. A whisper of milk.
My morning, held in porcelain—
warm, not too sweet.

This silence we share
is not empty.
It is full.

The scrape of a chair on the floor,
your yawn sounds like
the key turning in the lock.
Home.

You read. I write.
Worlds build and break
on either side of the wood,
but under it, our feet touch.

A secret that became a language.
A comma in our shared sentence.
This is the love that comes after the poetry.
This is the love that is the poetry—
the kind you live instead of just writing.

Not the fire, but the hearth.
The ordinary, breathtaking,
everyday magic of being known

# புரிதல்

நீ பேசாமல் இருக்கும் போது
உன் கண்கள் என்ன சொல்ல
விரும்புகின்றன என்று
இப்போது எனக்குத் தெரியும்.

நீ சிரிக்கும் போது
எந்த சிரிப்பு உண்மையானது,
எது மறைக்கும் முகமூடி என்று
நான் கற்றுக்கொண்டேன்.

உன் பயங்களை நான் அறிவேன்—
நீ யாரிடமும் சொல்லாதவை.
உன் கனவுகளை நான் அறிவேன்—
நீ தானே மறந்துவிட்ட கனவுகளை கூட.

காதல் என்பது வெறும் உணர்வு மட்டும்
அல்ல.
இது ஒருவரை மெதுவாக, அடுக்கு அடுக்காக,
வலி மற்றும் அழகுடன், தெரிந்துகொள்வது.

நீ என்னை முழுமையாக அறிவாய்.
நான் உன்னை முழுமையாக அறிவேன்.
இதுவே காதல் என்றால்,
நான் சரியாகவே செய்து வருகிறேன்.

# Lie to me

Lie to me.

Tell me we will be forever,
enjoying the bessy breeze,
roaming the city
riding our bicycles...

Tell me you won't let me go,
holding my hand,
locking our eyes
sharing our breath.

Tell me I'm enough, this
not so funny jokes,
non-stop geeky talks
and my sweet coo.

Tell me we will be alright,
sharing the candies,
meeting at our own ease
sleeping in peace...

# From up above

A friend like you is hard to find,
one who touches you deep inside.
You've given me the strength to carry on,
you've offered your hand to hold on.
When times are tough, I know you're there
to provide support and show you care.

If not for you, I would have drowned,
but you help keep me on solid ground.
I believe you were sent from the man above
because he knows the strength of your love.
You show that love in so many ways.
It helps me get through my darkest days.

I could skip a heartbeat, and I would survive,
I could be in a car crash and still be alive.
The clouds could fall out of the sky,
The oceans could disappear,
and the world turns dry.

These things in life are all bad, I know,
but there are far worse things,
just thought you should know.

Life would not be the same without someone like you.
You're there when I need you to help me through.
Through the good times and through the bad,
Be it happy, or be it sad.

I don't have to be with you to know you're there.
We don't have to see each other to know that we care.
We could be apart for years in the end,
and still remain the best of friends.

Life goes on, and people change,
And through it all, our friendship shall remain the same.
That's such a life, and how things come to be.

Just thought you should know,
how much you mean to me..
So, for that, I write this poem for you
and tell you from my heart, THANK YOU!

# The first crack

Before tonight,
we had no words for this.
Our love was soft mornings.
Gentle hands.

Then, the air split like glass.
You said things you didn't mean.
And I said things I did.

And in the silence,
we saw it,
the fear.

The kind of love that leaves bruises.
The map of where we could go wrong.
We just stood there,
breathing,
in the wreckage.

Then your hand reached.
Softer, this time.
I held on.
Learning how to break.
And still choose to stay.

# After the storm

I'm sorry.

Not because I have to say it,
but because I mean it
in the marrow of my bones.

I'm sorry for the words
that came out sharper
than I intended.

For the way I forgot
that your anger
is just fear wearing armor.

You looked at me differently today—
like I was capable
of breaking what we built.

And maybe I am.
Maybe we both are.

But here's the thing—
I don't want to be right.
I just want to be yours.

So let me hold you now,
not to erase the fight,
but to remind us both
that love is not about
never falling apart.

It's about choosing,
again and again,
to put each other
back together.

# Not my Kind

I am held in a
kind love.
It is sunlight through a window.
It is the ground after the storm.

There are no slammed doors here.
No bruises.
And I am grateful.

But,
this is not the love
that answers the ghosts
pacing the floors of my chest.

I am tired of a love
that is only peace.
I want the one
that is also a challenge.

I don't want a hand that just holds.
I want the one that grips.
That claims.
That knows I am not a paper boat,
to be folded gently.

Their eyes are calm.
And I am so safe there.
But I ache for the look
that burns.

The one that sees
the dark I'm hiding in
and says,
finally.

# The Distance Between Us

It didn't happen all at once.

There was no fight,
no betrayal,
no moment I could point to and say,
"That's where it broke."
It was quieter than that.

Like the way winter arrives—
not with thunder, but with mornings
that grow colder
without asking permission.

You stopped texting first.
I stopped asking how your day was.

We still said "I love you,"
but it started to sound
like a promise we made
to someone we used to be.

I don't know when
you became a stranger
I share a bed with.

But tonight,
lying next to you,
I felt the distance
wider than any ocean.

And I wondered—
when did we stop trying
to close it?

# நீ உதிர்த்த முதல் சொல்லாய் நான்

தவழும் வயதில் நீ தாவி அணைப்பவளாய்
நான் இருந்திருக்க வேண்டும்.
நீ மழலை மொழியில் உதிர்த்த
முதல் சொல்லாய்
நான் இருந்திருக் வேண்டும்.

முதல் நாள் பள்ளிக்குச் செல்லும் போது
நீ சிந்திய கண்ணீர் என்னுடயதாய்
வேண்டும்.
வீடு திரும்பியதும் நீ அணைக்கத் தேடுபவள்
நானாக வேண்டும்.

உனது கஸ்டங்கள் பகிரும் முதற்தோழியாய்
நான் நின்றிருக்க வேண்டும்.
உனக்குத் தலை வாரி ஒப்பனை
செய்பவளாய்
நான் இருந்திருக்க வேண்டும்.

சிசுவாய் உன்னை சுமந்தவளாய்
நான் பிறந்திருக்க வேண்டும்.
உனது கண்டிப்பான தாயாக
நான் பிறப்பெடுத்திருக்க வேண்டுமடி...

# We need to talk

Four words.
The sound of a song stopping mid-verse.
We sat. And for the first time,
looking at you felt like holding fire.

Your voice was a soft thing.
Breaking, but certain.
"I love you. But we are holding on to
what we were. Not what we are."

My mouth filled with arguments.
"No. We can fix this. Stay."
But the truth was a third person in the room.
Heavy. Quiet. Real.

We were just two people
loving the ghosts of who we used to be.
So I nodded. You cried.
I held your hand one last time.

And that was it.
No anger. No slamming doors. No wreckage.
Just the quiet, aching truth.
That sometimes, love is not enough.

# The Kindest Ending

We did not burn.
We folded —
like paper boats
when the tide changed.

No storms.
No slammed doors.
Just the soft undoing
of what we thought might last.

And still —
I am grateful.

For the laughter that hung between us
like summer clothes on a line.
For the mornings
you were my first light.

And though we are done,
I hope your skies stay kind,
your coffee stays warm,
and your heart finds someone
who doesn't flinch at its softness.

You were a chapter,
not a mistake.

And this —
this is not bitterness.

It's just love,
leaving
with both hands open.

# (By the one who left)

I loved you.
God, I did.

But love isn't always enough.
It's not a balm. It's a flame
that burns too long
and leaves you colder in the end.

You were the fire I wanted
even as it blistered my skin.

But I left —
not because I stopped loving you,
but because love started costing
more than it gave.

I left because sometimes
love is the most exquisite way
to fall apart.

# (By the one who was left behind)

You said you loved me —
and maybe you did.
But your love had edges,
sharp enough to bleed me
even as I held it close.

You walked away like it was mercy.
But mercy doesn't echo like this.
It doesn't haunt every quiet room.

I wasn't asking for perfect.
Just for you to choose me
when it got hard.

But you didn't.
You chose silence. You chose the door.

Now I sleep with the fire
you left in my chest
and the frost
your goodbye became.

# I miss you

Let me say it without the edges.
Without the guilt. Without the anger.

This is not an accusation.
It is not a wound
I am asking you to heal.
It is not a problem I am asking you to solve.

Do not tell me it will be alright.
Do not feel the weight of my sadness.
This is just the shape of things.
You, there. Me, here.

My hands are a little empty.
My heart is a little sad.
And it is okay.

This is not a storm.
It is not a breakdown.
It is just a fact. A truth.

I miss you. That is all.
I just wanted you to know.

# காய்ந்திடா கண்ணீர்

சோகம் களைந்து வாழ்தேன் உன்னால்
என்றே கூறித் தலையில் சுமந்தாய்
கறுத்துகள் நம்மில் வேறுபட்டு நின்றாலும்
பிரியேன் ஒருபோதும் உன்னை என்றாய்

என் வாழ்வே நீதான் எந்நாளும் நீதான்
என்றே நானும் வானில் மிதக்க
வாழ்வேன் நன்றாய் நீ இல்லை என்றால்
என்றே சொல்லிச் சிதரடித்தாய் என்னை
ஏனோ

நாம் சென்ற பாதைகள் நம் முகத்தை
மறந்தாலும்
நாம் கொண்ட தேடல்கள் நடுவழியில்
தவித்தாலும்
நாம் வாழ்ந்த காலங்கள் கனவாக
மறைந்தாலும்
கடைசியில் அழுத கண்ணீர் மட்டும் கைகளில்
இன்னும் ஒட்டுதடி...

# The Rage

I am on fire.
Not the kind that yells.
The kind that sits in the stomach.
Quiet. And burns.

I am on fire because you promised forever.
Then you left when 'forever' got hard.

I am on fire because I gave you
my softest parts.
And you held them like they were easy to replace.
You are probably fine.

I am here.
Trying to build a life in the crater you left.

I want to hate you.
God, I try.
But I can't. I still love you.
Even in this fire. And that —
That is the real rage.

# Maybe Tomorrow

You'll text me tomorrow.
I know you will.

You'll say you made a mistake,
that you miss me,
that you want to try again.
And I'll say the mistake is mine.
Of course I will.

Because this—
this silence, this ending—
it doesn't make sense.

So I'll wait.
I'll keep my phone close,
check it every five minutes,
rehearse what I'll say
when you finally call.

I'll wait.
Because love like ours doesn't just end.
It can't... Right?

# Sorry (But Not Really)

I know you hate this.
This need to give the ache a name.
To pin our ghosts to the page.

You want it silent.
A door, locked.
But I keep walking back.
Tracing the shape of us.
All the stages. All my mistakes.

This isn't for you. Not anymore.
This is for me.
This is how I clear my thoughts.
How I find the wound and finally let it close.

I have to write it to make it real.
And then I have to write it to make it done.
This is how I get over us.
I had to.

# Loved you first

She'll try so damn hard to fix your broken heart;
but it'll bleed in the ink I versed.

She'll give you oceans of love;
yet you'll die of my thirst

For this isn't just a poem, my love

This is a curse;
of the woman who loved you first.

# If I'd only known

If I'd only known,
That this is the last time we've met,
I would have stopped the break of dawn,
And stopped the sun from setting.

If I'd only known,
That I wouldn't ever see you again,
I would have framed a picture of you within,
To end my suffering, to end my pain.

If I'd only known,
That this is the last time I sit by your side,
I would have told you how much I loved you,
Keeping other things aside.

If I'd only known,
That we would never hold hands again,
I would have held them strong,
And never let anything go wrong.

If I'd only known,
That you would always stand by my side,
I would have fought the world for you,
Breaking all the walls through.

If I'd only known,
That your love was true,
If I'd only known that you would come back soon,
I would have waited for you to come by..

If I'd only known any of this,
That you were what I was breathing for,
I would have breathed my last for you,
Seen you enough and bid you adieu.

While all I can do now,
Is sit here, wait
and love you.

# Hello Best Friend

Hello best friend to whom I fell
Long time no see, I hope you're well
If not, don't hide, I will smell
Have a look, it's where I dwell
Since you left, it's no better than hell
Do come fast, need a tight hug-shell
Life was greater under your spell
Just don't miss, I have a story to tell
But make sure your eyes don't well
Hello best friend to whom I fell.

# This is it?

My hand did not reach for the phone this morning.
I made coffee. I watched the sun.
And I thought of you.
Of course.

But the thought did not arrive like a wound.
It didn't break anything.
It was just soft.
The echo of a dream
I used to have.

I don't know if I am 'over you.'
(I don't know what that means.)
But the love is no longer a ghost pacing my chest.
It is no longer a rage.

It is just a chapter.
A lesson. A page I am finally turning.
I am learning to be my own light.
And maybe that is enough.

# Thank you

You taught me
love is not ownership.
You taught me
I could feel so deeply.
Recklessly.
The part of me that burns.

Thank you for the mornings.
For the quiet that sounded like home.
And thank you for leaving.
For knowing staying would have been
just a different way to break us.

Some love is not 'forever.'
It is a lesson.
It teaches you how to be brave
the next time.

So, thank you.
For the love. For the pain.

Thank you for the person
I became after.
You are not a regret.

You are a chapter
I am grateful I got to write.

Goodbye.
Not with bitterness.
With gratitude.

You were my everything.
Now, you are a memory I hold gently.
A lesson I will carry for the rest of my life.

# முற்றும்

நான் ஒரு கவிஞன் அல்ல என்று
நினைத்தேன்
உன்னை சந்திக்கும் வரை.
என் வாழ்வில் ஒளி இல்லை என்று
நினைத்தேன்
நீ புன்னகைக்கும் வரை.

காதல் என்பது எளிதானது என்று
நினைத்தேன்
நீ போகும் வரை.
வலி என்பது என்னை உடைக்கும் என்று
நினைத்தேன்
நான் மீண்டும் எழும் வரை.

உன் நினைவுகள் என்னை விட்டு போகும்
என்று நினைத்தேன்
ஆனால் அவை என் பாடல்களாக மாறின.
நீ என் முடிவு அல்ல. நீ என் ஆரம்பம்.

காதலிக்க தெரிந்தவன்.
வலியை தாங்க தெரிந்தவன்.
எழுத தெரிந்தவன்.
மீண்டும் வாழ தெரிந்தவன்.

நீ போனாலும்,
நான் இங்கே இருக்கிறேன்.
முழுமையாக.
உடைந்திருந்தாலும் முழுமையாக.

நீ எனக்கு கற்றுக்கொடுத்த பாடங்களுடன்,
நீ விட்டுச்சென்ற காதலுடன்,
நீ எழுதி வைத்த கவிதைகளுடன்.

"நீ, நான், மற்றும் நடுவில் இருந்த
அனைத்தும்."

நன்றி.
பிரியாவிடை முற்றும்.

www.ingramcontent.com/pod-product-compliance
Lightning Source LLC
Chambersburg PA
CBHW060348050426
42449CB00011B/2868